D1190272

COUNTRY PROFILES

SOMALIA

BY GOLRIZ GOLKAR

BELLWETHER MEDIA • MINNEAPOLIS, MN

Blastoff! Discovery launches a new mission: reading to learn. Filled with facts and features, each book offers you an exciting new world to explore!

BLASTOFF! UNIVERSE

BLASTOFF! Beginners — GRADE K

BLASTOFF! READERS — GRADES 1-3

BLASTOFF! DISCOVERY — GRADE 4

This edition first published in 2022 by Bellwether Media, Inc.

No part of this publication may be reproduced in whole or in part without written permission of the publisher.
For information regarding permission, write to Bellwether Media, Inc., Attention: Permissions Department,
6012 Blue Circle Drive, Minnetonka, MN 55343.

Library of Congress Cataloging-in-Publication Data

Names: Golkar, Golriz, author.
Title: Somalia / by Golriz Golkar.
Other titles: Blastoff! discovery. Country profiles.
Description: Minneapolis, MN : Bellwether Media, Inc., 2022. | Series: Blastoff! Discovery. Country profiles | Includes bibliographical references and index. | Audience: Ages 7-13 | Audience: Grades 4-6 | Summary: "Engaging images accompany information about Somalia. The combination of high-interest subject matter and narrative text is intended for students in grades 3 through 8"–Provided by publisher.
Identifiers: LCCN 2021051760 (print) | LCCN 2021051761 (ebook) | ISBN 9781644876145 (library binding) | ISBN 9781648346255 (ebook)
Subjects: LCSH: Somalia–Juvenile literature.
Classification: LCC DT401.5 .G65 2022 (print) | LCC DT401.5 (ebook) | DDC 967.73–dc23/eng/20211022
LC record available at https://lccn.loc.gov/2021051760
LC ebook record available at https://lccn.loc.gov/2021051761

Editor: Kieran Downs   Designer: Brittany McIntosh

Printed in the United States of America, North Mankato, MN.

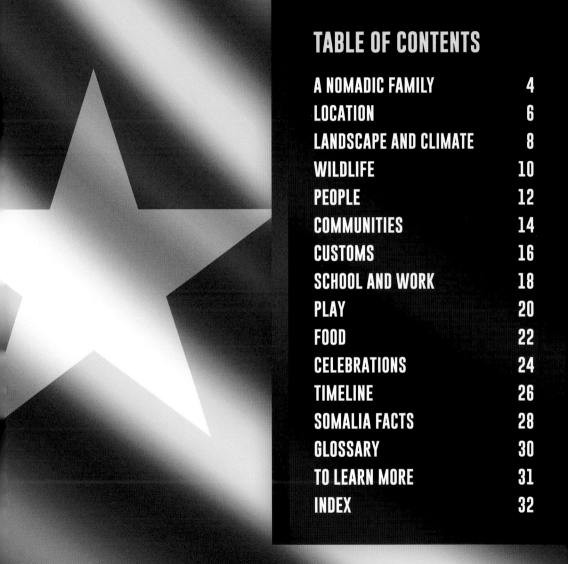

TABLE OF CONTENTS

A **nomadic** Somali family wakes to a bright sunrise. They enjoy camel milk and grains for breakfast. Next, they take down their *aqal*. This hut is made from animal skins and branches. The family gathers their goats and camels. They roll the hut and place it on a camel's back. It is time to move again.

OTHER TOP SITES

LAAS GEEL

MOGADISHU CATHEDRAL

SA'AD AD-DIN ISLANDS

ZEILA

The family travels the **plains**. They search for water and grass for their animals. They eat dried meats as they walk. By evening, they find a place to set up their hut. They build a fire at sunset. This is just one of the rich and fascinating **cultures** of Somalia!

Somalia is located in eastern Africa. It is part of the Horn of Africa **peninsula**. Its southernmost tip crosses over the **equator**. Somalia covers 246,201 square miles (637,657 square kilometers). Mogadishu, the capital, lies in the south, along the eastern coast.

Kenya meets Somalia's southwestern border. Somalia wraps around its western neighbor, Ethiopia. Somalia's small northwestern border touches Djibouti. The **Gulf** of Aden borders Somalia to the north. The waters of the Indian Ocean touch the eastern coast.

KENYA

GULF OF
ADEN

DJIBOUTI

BERBERA

- - - HARGEISA

ETHIOPIA

SOMALIA

INDIAN
OCEAN

MOGADISHU

MARKA

N
W ╬ E
S

INDEPENDENT SOMALILAND

Part of northern Somalia, called
Somaliland, declared itself
independent from the rest of the
country. However, most of the world
still considers it part of Somalia.

LANDSCAPE AND CLIMATE

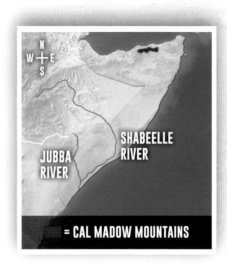

Sandy coastal plains stretch across northern Somalia to the coast. The Cal Madow mountains run through the north, peaking at Mount Shimbiris. The Hawd **Plateau** stands near the border with Ethiopia. Small shrubs and scattered trees dot its **savanna** landscape. Large hills stand over southern Somalia. **Fertile** valleys stretch between the Jubba and Shabeelle Rivers in the southwest. Sandy beaches line the eastern coast.

LONG BEACHES

Somalia has the longest coastline in mainland Africa.

GALGODON HIGHLANDS

MOGADISHU
Average
seasonal highs
and lows

JANUARY
HIGH: 88 °F (31 °C)
LOW: 76 °F (24 °C)

APRIL
HIGH: 89 °F (32 °C)
LOW: 80 °F (27 °C)

JULY
HIGH: 83 °F (28 °C)
LOW: 76 °F (24 °C)

OCTOBER
HIGH: 86 °F (30 °C)
LOW: 77 °F (25 °C)

°F = degrees Fahrenheit
°C = degrees Celsius

Inland Somalia is hot and dry. Coastal areas are
more **humid**. A heavy rainy season occurs from April
to June. Lighter rain falls from October to December.

9

WILDLIFE

Somalia is home to many wild animals. Leopards, the national animal of Somalia, roam the plains. They hunt gazelles and silver dik-diks. Rüppell's foxes chase lizards across rocks. Somali sand boas slither through sandy shrublands. They search for Somali golden moles. Bengal snappers and giant manta rays swim in the coastal waters.

Many birds call Somalia home. Ash's larks and Obbia larks build nests in grassland shrubs. Somali pigeons wander the dry coastal regions. Somali thrushes sing in the mountains. Archer's buzzards soar in the skies searching for prey.

GAZELLE

BENGAL SNAPPERS

RÜPPELL'S FOX

GIANT MANTA RAY

LEOPARD

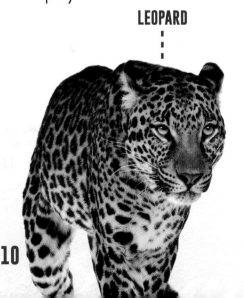

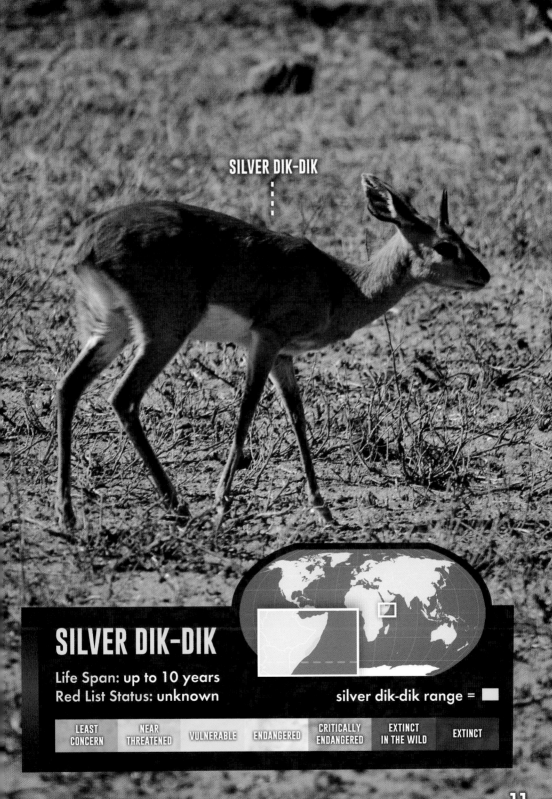

SILVER DIK-DIK

SILVER DIK-DIK

Life Span: up to 10 years
Red List Status: unknown

silver dik-dik range = ▇

LEAST CONCERN	NEAR THREATENED	VULNERABLE	ENDANGERED	CRITICALLY ENDANGERED	EXTINCT IN THE WILD	EXTINCT

PEOPLE

LANGUAGES

Somalia's past settlers have affected the country's spoken languages. Many Somalis also speak English and Italian. University classes are often taught in these languages in addition to Somali.

Somalia is home to more than 12 million people. More than 8 out of 10 people have Somali roots. They are related to Somali tribes living all over the Horn of Africa. Other **ethnic** groups in Somalia include the Arab, Bantu, Bajun, and Bravanese peoples.

Nearly all Somali people are Sunni Muslim. A very small number practice other types of Islam. Somalia has two official languages. Somali is one of them. Several Somali **dialects** are spoken. Arabic is officially spoken in northern and coastal regions.

FAMOUS FACE

Name: Iman
Birthday: July 25, 1955
Hometown: Mogadishu, Somalia
Famous for: World-famous supermodel dedicated to helping end poverty in Africa and improving educational opportunities for young women

SPEAK SOMALI

ENGLISH	SOMALI	HOW TO SAY IT
hello	as-salamu alaykum	ah-sah-LAHM ah-LAY-koom
goodbye	nabad gelyo	nah-bawd geh-LEE-oh
please	fadlan	FAD-lahn
thank you	mahadsanid	mah-HAHD-sah-ned
yes	haa	HAA
no	maya	ma-YA

MOGADISHU

HARGEISA

Nearly half of all Somalis live in **urban** areas. Many live in coastal towns. Other Somalis live in the northwest and southern regions. Brick or wooden houses are common. Buses and trucks help people get around town.

Many Somalis are nomads. They move around **rural** areas where crops and animals can get water from rain, wells, and rivers. They make huts from animal hides. Settled rural residents live in small houses or tree branch huts. Homes often lack running water or electricity. Rural Somalis often travel on foot or by donkey, camel, or cattle.

CLANS

Somalis generally belong to one of five large clans. Each clan is divided into smaller ones.

NOMADS

Somalis wash their hands in a bowl of water before eating. Men and women often eat separately. They gather around one large plate of food. Men are usually served first. Women and children are served second.

Somalis enjoy **traditional** music and dance. Song lyrics are typically poems. Flute, drum, and horn music plays as poems are sung. Dancers wear colorful clothing. They dance in lines or circles to songs and drum music. *Dhaanto* is a popular dance that imitates camel movements. *Jaandheer* is a lively step dance enjoyed at weddings.

PUBLIC SCHOOLS

A lack of teachers, materials, and space have closed all public schools in Somalia. International aid groups run many private schools.

Less than half of all children in Somalia attend school. Boys are more likely to attend. Some urban Somali children attend private schools. Many rural children work instead of attending school. Groups are working to make education available to everybody. Primary education lasts for eight years. Secondary education lasts for four years. Some Somalis attend university. Others attend technical or agricultural schools.

Most Somalis farm to survive. They grow crops such as grains or corn. Some Somalis raise animals. Sheep, goats, and cattle are all common. Other Somalis work on farms or large **plantations**. Bananas, sugarcane, and rice are grown there. Others work in office jobs or the fishing industry.

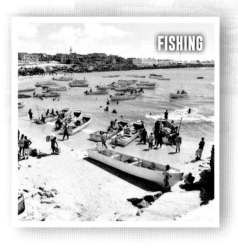

FISHING

FARMING

19

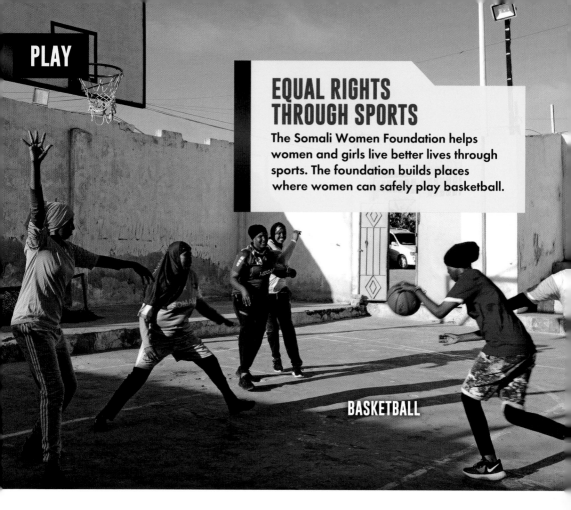

EQUAL RIGHTS THROUGH SPORTS

The Somali Women Foundation helps women and girls live better lives through sports. The foundation builds places where women can safely play basketball.

BASKETBALL

Soccer is a popular sport in Somalia. Somalis enjoy watching national soccer clubs compete. Basketball and volleyball are other favorite team sports. Men and children mainly play sports in Somalia. Cultural rules do not allow women to play organized games. However, some Somali women still play soccer and basketball for fun.

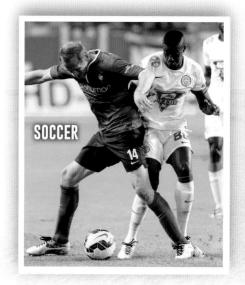

SOCCER

Somalis enjoy activities such as swimming and cycling. Gardening and fishing are also popular. Dominoes and chess are enjoyed throughout the country. Women often enjoy making handmade objects. They weave clothes, fans, and crafts.

WEAVING

HENNA HANDS

Henna dye is used to decorate hands in many Asian and African countries, including Somalia. Try making your own designs!

What You Need:
- white paper
- brown markers

How to Play:
1. Trace one or both of your hands on white paper.
2. Create traditional designs such as flowers, leaves, dots, swirls, diamonds, and zigzags. Be as creative as you like. You may check the internet for pictures of real henna drawings. Try to copy the designs you find!
3. Display your artwork on a wall when you are done!

MAKING ANJERO

Rice and millet are **staples** throughout Somalia. Breakfast may include thin millet pancakes called *anjero*. They may be dusted with sugar. *Sabaayad* is a flatbread that can be eaten with any meal. Urban Somalis may eat *bariis iskukaris* for lunch. This spicy rice is mixed with small pieces of meat or vegetables. Coastal Somalis enjoy fried fish. Dinners are usually light. Spicy bean dishes such as *cambuulo* are eaten with tomatoes and herbs.

Milk is a staple for nomadic Somalis. Goats and camels provide milk for drinks and yogurt. Nomads also eat some grains and preserved meats.

SABAAYAD

BARIIS ISKUKARIS

KAC KAC (SOMALI DOUGHNUTS)

These soft doughnuts are often enjoyed with tea or coffee.

Ingredients:
2 cups flour
1/2 cup sugar
1 teaspoon baking powder
2 large eggs
1/2 cup melted unsalted butter
2 tablespoons warm milk
vegetable oil for frying

Steps:
1. Mix the flour, sugar, and baking powder in a bowl.

2. Add the melted butter and mix well.

3. Lightly beat the eggs and add to the dough along with the milk.

4. Knead the dough with your hands for 3 minutes. Let the dough rest for 10 minutes.

5. Roll out the dough to a 1/4-inch (1/2-centimeter) thickness.

6. Cut the dough into about 24 pieces.

7. With an adult's help, fry the doughnut pieces in hot vegetable oil for three to four minutes or until golden brown.

8. Let the doughnuts cool and enjoy!

CELEBRATIONS

Some Somalis celebrate *Dab Shiid* in March. They jump over fires and welcome the arrival of Persian New Year. Somalis also celebrate many Muslim holidays. They **fast** during the month of Ramadan. They only eat and drink while the sun is set. They visit **mosques** and help people in need.

At the end of Ramadan, Somalis celebrate *Eid-al-Fitr*. They feast and exchange gifts with family and friends. Children may receive new clothes. Somalis celebrate *Eid al-Adha* by fasting the day before. They attend mosques and gather with friends and family. Together, they celebrate their rich culture!

EID AL-ADHA

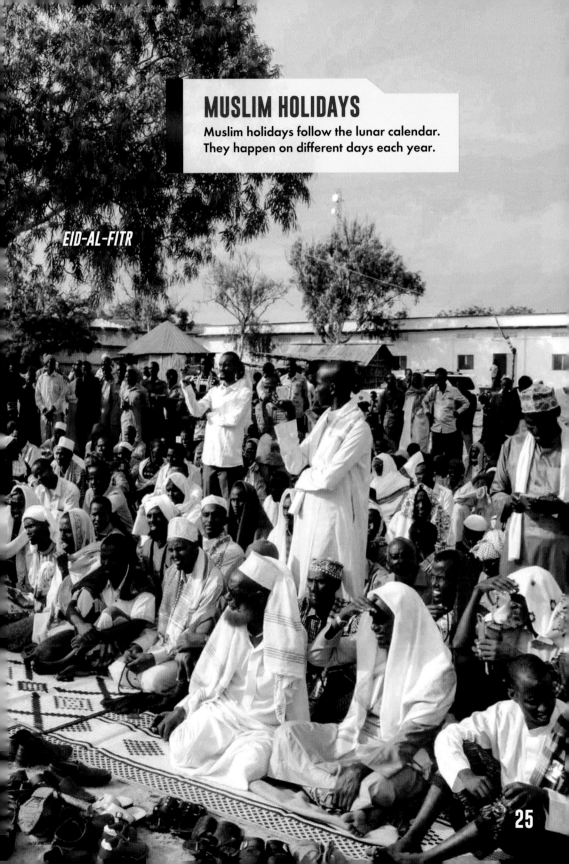

MUSLIM HOLIDAYS

Muslim holidays follow the lunar calendar. They happen on different days each year.

EID-AL-FITR

TIMELINE

1960
The British and Italian parts of Somalia become independent and form the United Republic of Somalia

AROUND 1300
Arab tribes create the Sultanate of Adal near the Gulf of Aden

1800s
France, England, and Italy overtake what will eventually become Somalia

AROUND 1575
The Sultanate of Adal splits into smaller states

1969
General Siad Barre overthrows the government to become president and establish a socialist state

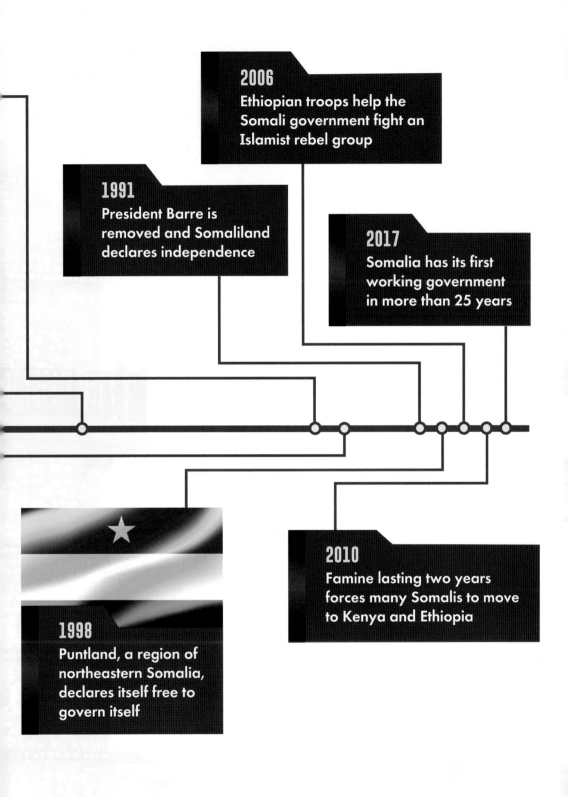

2006
Ethiopian troops help the Somali government fight an Islamist rebel group

1991
President Barre is removed and Somaliland declares independence

2017
Somalia has its first working government in more than 25 years

2010
Famine lasting two years forces many Somalis to move to Kenya and Ethiopia

1998
Puntland, a region of northeastern Somalia, declares itself free to govern itself

SOMALIA FACTS

Official Name: Federal Republic of Somalia

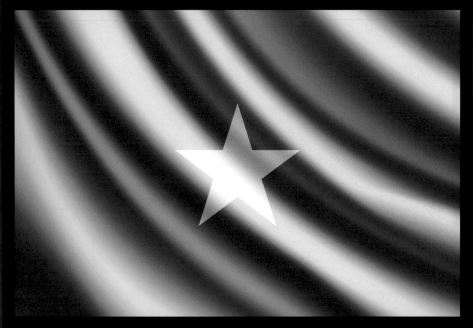

Flag of Somalia: The Somali flag is light blue. A white, five-pointed star sits in the center. The blue represents the sky and the Indian Ocean. The five points of the star represent the five regions in the Horn of Africa where Somali people live.

Area: 246,201 square miles
(637,657 square kilometers)

Capital City: Mogadishu

Important Cities: Hargeisa, Marka, Berbera

Population:
12,094,640 (July 2021)

COUNTRYSIDE
53.3%

WHERE
PEOPLE LIVE

CITY
46.7%

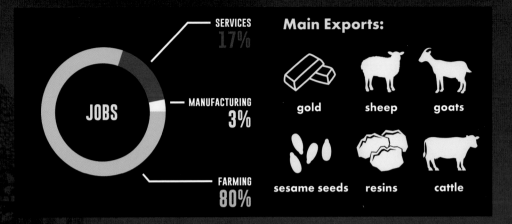

SERVICES
17%

JOBS

MANUFACTURING
3%

FARMING
80%

Main Exports:

gold   sheep   goats

sesame seeds   resins   cattle

National Holiday:
Republic Day (July 1)

Main Languages:
Somali (official), Arabic (official)

Form of Government:
federal parliamentary republic

Title for Country Leaders:
president (head of state), prime minister (head of government)

SUNNI
MUSLIM
100%

RELIGION

Unit of Money:
Somali shilling

GLOSSARY

cultures—beliefs, arts, and ways of life in places or societies

dialects—local ways of speaking particular languages

equator—an imaginary circle around the Earth equally distant from the north and south poles

ethnic—related to a group of people who share customs and an identity

fast—to stop eating all foods or particular foods for a time

fertile—able to support growth

gulf—part of an ocean or sea that extends into land

humid—having a lot of moisture in the air

mosques—buildings that Muslims use for worship

nomadic—relating to people who have no fixed home, but wander from place to place

peninsula—a section of land that extends out from a larger piece of land and is almost completely surrounded by water

plains—large areas of flat land

plantations—large farms that grow coffee beans, cotton, rubber, or other crops; plantations are mainly found in warm climates.

plateau—an area of flat, raised land

rural—related to the countryside

savanna—an African grassland containing scattered trees

staples—widely used foods or other items

traditional—related to customs, ideas, or beliefs handed down from one generation to the next

urban—related to cities and city life

TO LEARN MORE

AT THE LIBRARY

Barghoorn, Linda. *A Refugee's Journey from Somalia (Leaving My Homeland)*. New York, N.Y.: Crabtree Publishing Company, 2018.

Hassig, Susan M. *Somalia*. New York, N.Y.: Cavendish Square Publishing, 2017.

Rechner, Amy. *Kenya*. Minneapolis, Minn.: Bellwether Media, 2019.

ON THE WEB

FACTSURFER

Factsurfer.com gives you a safe, fun way to find more information.

1. Go to www.factsurfer.com.

2. Enter "Somalia" into the search box and click 🔍.

3. Select your book cover to see a list of related content.

INDEX

The images in this book are reproduced through the courtesy of: MDart10, front cover, pp. 9 (Mogadishu), 13 (Mogadishu); Mike Goldwater/ Alamy Stock Photo, pp. 4-5; Victor Modesto, p. 5 (LaasGeel); omar degan, p. 5 (Mogadishu Cathedral); Lakmi00/ Wikimedia Commons, p. 5 (Sa'ad ad-Din Islands); ERIC LAFFORGUE/ Alamy Stock Photo, p. 5 (Zelia); Kalik Ahmed, p. 8; Andrew Palmer/ Alamy Stock Photo, p. 9 (Galgodon Mountains); Eric Isselee, p. 10 (leopard); ChWeiss, p. 10 (gazelle); WaterFrame/ Alamy Stock Photo, p. 10 (Bengal snappers); Henri Martin, p. 10 (Rüppell's fox); Paola Ruffo Ruffo, p. 10 (giant manta ray); HelgeNeven, pp. 10-11 (silver dik-dik); afad tuncay, p. 12; Ron Adar, p. 13 (Iman); robertharding/ Alamy Stock Photo, p. 14; Mike Goldwater/ Alamy Stock Photo, p. 15; REUTERS/ Alamy Stock Photo, pp. 16, 17, 20 (basketball), 22, 24 (*Eid al-Adha*); Free Wind 2014, p. 18; Xinhua/ Alamy Stock Photo, p. 19 (fishing); Mark Pearson/ Alamy Stock Photo, p. 19 (farming); Laszlo Szirtesi/ Alamy Stock Photo, p. 20 (soccer); Liba Taylor/ Alamy Stock Photo, p. 21 (weaving); Eric Lafforgue/ Art in All of Us/ Getty Images, p. 21 (henna); Isa sora, p. 23 (*sabaayad*); Fanfo, p. 23 (*bariis iskukaris*); kMunge, p. 23 (kac kac); Africa Collection/ Alamy Stock Photo, pp. 24-25 (*Eid al-Fitr*); Jean-Claude FRANCOLON/ Getty Images, p. 26; Oporty786, p. 27; Middayexpress/ Wikipedia, p. 29 (banknote); Nicholas Wright, p. 29 (coin).